DANCING WITH THE ANGELS

T0148364

OTHER BOOKS BY GRACE JOHNSTON

Celestial Inspirations – Thoughts Beyond the Intellect

Angels – Those Wondrous Beings

Our Creation and Destiny – Book

One – Charting the Heavens

Making the connection between science and spirituality

DANCING WITH THE ANGELS

A Light in Times of Darkness

Grace Johnston

iUniverse, Inc.
New York   Bloomington

DANCING WITH THE ANGELS

A Light in Times of Darkness

iUniverse books may be ordered through booksellers or by contacting:

iUniverse
1663 Liberty Drive
Bloomington, IN 47403
www.iuniverse.com
1-800-Authors (1-800-288-4677)

ISBN: 978-1-4401-0683-5 (pbk)
ISBN: 978-1-4401-0684-2 (ebk)

Library of Congress Control Number: 2008943552

Printed in the United States of America

iUniverse rev. date: 12/29/2008

THANK YOU

My many thanks go to all you wonderful friends and people who have encouraged and prodded me along the way. You have been so supportive and understanding of my efforts to complete this book and others I am creating.

More than anyone, my appreciation goes to my many angelic helpers who have gently but firmly helped me along the way, even when I have been at a loss for words, giving me through divine guidance the exact words to put in text. I have greatly disappointed them at times I am sure, with my procrastination, but as is ever the way with angels, they have never left me or given up on me. For that I am eternally grateful.

Table of Contents

INTRODUCTION

People everywhere are considering the existence of angelic beings and questioning their own beliefs. Do angels really exist or is it just a figment of imagination?

Throughout the centuries the presence of angels has been expressed through art and journalism. One only has to look through a museum or browse through an art book or the internet to see pictures of angels in every shape, form and description. Stories of encounters with angels are appearing more and more in magazines and books in bookstores throughout the world. People are expressing more openly their experiences and suspicions of encounters with angels.

Why have angels been appearing more in our awareness than previously?

Could it be that we have reached a period in our history that has brought about calls for help: the need for relief from the traumas and stress that originates from weather disasters, financial upheavals, medical and health worries, and, in general, tremendous challenges in every society all over the world.

People everywhere are searching for answers. Some are desperate to find relief to their stress.

Our Creator[1], being constantly tuned in to our needs, hears the cries of the people, and has provided for our needs.

In these days of turmoil one of the greatest aids to obtaining peace and happiness is the service of angels.

The presence of angels is more evident and active in the world, especially now as we prepare to evolve through a transition of both earthly and spiritual changes.

Understanding the information in this book will help you exist in a better manner and evolve more quickly through your existence, by bringing you closer to your angels. I hope that you will relate to this book purposefully and beneficially. I pray that it will help you create your own world of peace and love, and that you will share it with all whom you come in contact with. I pray that angels bring to every one of you who is reading this book their blessings, their love for you, and their healing power. I want each of you to receive some sort of personal gift from your angels.

Let me introduce you to Angels, some of the most marvelous creatures God ever created.

---

1   [1]The highest universal creative force is known by many names. History has provided us with: "Supreme Being, God, Father, The Highest One, The Creator, Lord, El Shaddai, Yahweh, etc." All are names given to the highest, supreme, primary creative force in order to identify something that is unidentifiable except through nature and in an intangible way. For purposes of clarity and simplification, in this book I will use the most popular usage of the name, "God," to represent this universal creative force.

CHAPTER 1 -

THE BEGINNING

I remember no childhood experiences with angels. All I knew about angels was what I'd read in books and specifically in the Bible. Raised in a small southern town, I had a very traditional mainstream Christian background. At Christmas time we always placed an angel on the top of our Christmas tree, and pictures and little statues of angels adorned our house. Sometimes the town displayed angels as a central theme in the seasonal decorations.

I still remember seeing a picture of a guardian angel watching over children crossing a bridge. It hung in our church Sunday School classroom. Whenever I did something risky or came close to having an accident, my mother used to tell me that my guardian angel had watched over me and kept me safe.

I didn't think much about angels back then, only occasionally having fleeting thoughts of them.

Many years ago something happened that convinced me that supernatural events take place in this world. It was during this event that I first became aware of the fact that there are beings around us that are not normally visible to us.

I was going through a very traumatic time – one of those times that come in almost everyone's life when nothing seems to go right and everything seems to go wrong. I struggled to find happiness, to find a way to resolve problems and make accurate decisions, which, in turn, affected my family. I felt like my world was crumbling around me and I didn't have anyone left to turn to for support or help.

Since I grew up with a Christian background, I turned to the only source of strength I knew— the local church. There, I met wonderful people who offered support and comfort that I soaked up like a sponge. I was invited to attend a Bible study group that met once a week. As homework assignments, we read passages or chapters in the Bible every day.

My greatest source of comfort soon sprang from my habit of reading the Bible early every morning. While I drank my morning coffee, I read and enjoyed my private time with God. Before long, I noticed that my days always seemed better because of it. Conversely, I also discovered that if I didn't read the Bible in the morning my day simply did not go as well.

One particular morning, stressed from a poor night's sleep, I pulled out my study Bible, The New Oxford Annotated Bible with the Apocrypha, Revised Standard Version. As I leafed through it looking for inspiration, the book slipped off my lap and landed on the floor. When I picked it up, I saw that it had opened to a chapter in the Apocrypha. Since I was not Catholic, I had never read it or even been interested in any of the other extra books in the Catholic Bible. However, something caught my eye and I started reading the Book of Tobit in the Apocrypha. That chapter of the Bible speaks of a demon, Asmodeous, and the angel Raphael. Every time the words Asmodeous and Raphael appeared, they showed up to me as if in big, bold text. For some reason I still can't explain, this both astonished and frightened me. Nothing of this nature had ever happened to me before, and

I felt that it was a sign from God, that God was trying to tell me something.

Then I recalled an event that took place about a month earlier that seemed to make it even more significant. In a phone conversation with a business acquaintance who was upset over what he thought was a bad business deal, he declared that a recent meeting had turned into a heated argument and someone called him Asmodeous. I thought it described a mood he was in or some sort of strange personality trait, but since I had never heard the word before, I asked him what it meant. He said it was the lowest, meanest, vilest thing on earth. Because this businessman had a reputation of having a violent temper on occasion, I discounted his complaint and immediately forgot about it – until today. As the realization of where I had heard the word before dawned on me, I was astounded (as if the distinctly bold text was not enough).

I ran to phone a friend from church, hoping to find out what she knew about this sort of experience happening to anyone else.

She helped me calm down, and then suggested I go to a church library to search for information that might help me. I went to the next town, to Saint Mary's Catholic College, which has a wonderful reference library. After asking the librarian to help me locate information on the two entities named in the book of Tobit, I discovered information on the identities of Asmodeous and Raphael. According to a book that listed angel hierarchy (I have forgotten which book it was), Asmodeous was an angel underneath Satan and Raphael was an archangel in the Holy realm.

Moreover, I also found a great amount of information about other angels. I spent the rest of the day reading about them.

I had a strong feeling that this was God's way of getting my attention, showing me that there is life beyond what is in our temporal vision.

As my spiritual life progressed, I continued to study and research spiritual and supernatural events.

Gathering more and more knowledge as years passed, I moved by choice from one metaphysical and supernatural experience to another. Since I had so many questions, I was always open to find answers on spiritual matters. In my prayers I asked that God lead me to what He wanted me to know. Before every church service and religious or spiritual seminar and group gathering, I prayed that God open my eyes and ears to only what He wanted me to know. I asked Jesus to be with me, to guide and protect me in every learning experience.

As far back as I can remember, I have always had a strong desire for knowledge, and have read extensively, studying many religions and scriptures. I questioned the existence of God and other spiritual beings in my youth. When I questioned ministers or my religious friends, they always told me that God and everything mentioned in the Bible was real, and that I just needed to take it all on faith and believe everything without asking further questions and without having to see proof.

Unfortunately, however, I couldn't believe something just because someone told me about it. With true doubt in my heart, I asked God to prove to me that he existed.

Over a short period of time he did just that.

Thus began a lifetime of events, which eventually proved to me that things happen in this world that our physical eyes and ears cannot see or hear, and that supernatural and metaphysical beings do exist.

CHAPTER 2 -

APPEARANCE OF AN ANGEL

My first vivid experience with an angel proved to me that angels are real.

Back in the late 1980's my world seemed to cave in on me. There were so many major concerns in my life: The company I worked for was going out of business and I was facing a job loss. I dreaded the change that would cause. What if I had to move? How would I pay moving expenses? Financial worries were eating at me. On top of this, my children had problems and so did my friends. My son had been recently diagnosed with a serious heart problem. My other son was in a forced job change and experiencing financial difficulties. I was concerned about my own health. I was experiencing strange pains and maladies that my doctor couldn't identify other than problems caused by stress. My mother was aging and becoming more dependent on me. One of my closest friends had died quite suddenly and unexpectedly, and another friend learned she had inoperable cancer.

I felt all these burdens like the weight of the world on my shoulders.

One morning I woke up so mentally and physically tired I started crying, and the tears would not stop. I was in such a deep depression that thinking clearly was difficult and making decisions became impossible. Before I knew it, I was thinking that I did not want to continue living. My thoughts then went to imagining what it would be like in heaven and the afterlife. Heaven sounded so wonderful and exactly where I wanted to be at that very instant. I felt hopeless and unhappy. I needed a way out.

With methodical determination, I planned how to kill myself, but decided not to because I feared pain, and also because I knew it would hurt my children if I committed suicide. In my search for a way out, I remembered the religious teachings of my youth. I tried reading the Bible and inspirational passages but could not concentrate enough to absorb what I was reading. I tried praying for God to lift this depression from me, but nothing seemed to help. Then I started to pray that God go ahead and take me, but I remembered that I had to go see my mother. I knew my departure from this earth would have to wait until I returned home that afternoon, because my mother was depending on me run an errand for her, and I needed to complete that task. My immediate concern was that my mother not know how badly I felt and how depressed I was. I didn't feel strong enough to deal with her reaction. Again I prayed to God for strength and to remove the sad and hopeless feeling. Finally, I was able to think clearly enough to call a friend.

"Can you help me? Will you pray for me? I've just got to get through this day, 'cause I've got to go see my mother and I'm feeling so bad, and I can't stop crying, and I don't know what's wrong with me, and...." I heard myself babbling in desperation.

My friend answered, "Come on over."

I stumbled around, found my car keys and purse, and drove over to her house, praying that I would have a clear enough mind to drive safely and not hurt anyone.

My friend and I tried to pray, but because she didn't understand fully what was going on inside me, she wasn't sure what to pray for. I didn't know how to pray because I was too upset and depressed to talk to God. Mostly we just sat in silence trying to feel the presence of God, while waiting for direction and help through the Holy Spirit.

Finally, I said, "God, help me."

After a few moments of silence, I sensed someone standing behind me. Seconds later, I felt a very large presence wrap itself around me in a gentle but firm hug. I couldn't physically see anything, despite the fact that I was very aware that I was being held. I knew instantly and without a doubt that it was an angel. I could see it in my mind's eye, and feel the presence – a very strong yet gentle sensation, like thick white fog with form.

I spoke, in pleasant surprise, "An angel is giving me a hug. I can sense and feel and see it in my mind." My friend who sat across from me looked up and smiled. She said. "I can see lots of small angels dancing all around you and over your head."

She quietly considered this, and then said, "This is really beautiful. I see your angels and they are dancing all around you. They're small, because they have to be small to all be in this room, but I can see them."

I couldn't see the tiny dancing angels, but I definitely felt that angel around me, still hugging me, like a huge form or mass of energy enfolding me.

I questioned my friend about what she was seeing. She said, "I can't see the large angel around you, but I know it is here."

Suddenly the feelings of depression disappeared. I was filled with a feeling of total love and joy, an emotion so wonderful I couldn't think of words adequate enough to describe it. I was overflowing with ecstasy. Peaceful and happy again, I now no longer wanted to die.

My friend and I talked about what had happened, and by the time I left her house I felt confident and strong enough to deal with anything. I was cheerful and filled with love. It was a miracle.

I went on with my day in a pleasant and peaceful mood, the presence of the large angel vivid in my mind. The wonderful feeling of joy and peace stayed with me for days. Even though I don't always feel those same strong feelings in my everyday life, I still remember the appearance of the angel and its love for me.

Since that awesome experience, angels have continued to attract and fascinate me. And I've learned that I am not the only one who has had visits with an angel.

CHAPTER 3 -

FORMATION OF BELIEFS

St. Thomas Aquinas (1225 or 1227 – 1274), the Patron Saint of Catholic universities and schools, in <u>The Summa Theologica of St. Thomas Aquinas</u>, said "Angels transcend every religion, every philosophy, every creed. In fact angels have no religion as we know it ... their existence precedes every religious system that has ever existed on earth."

Many great philosophers and religious leaders have spoken of angels as realities. Emanuel Swedenborg, philosopher and scientist (1688-1772), in his book <u>Conversations with Angels: What Swedenborg Heard in Heaven</u>, spoke of visiting the Other World and conversing with the angels.

The belief in angels is as varied as there are different religions or belief systems. Religions over hundreds and thousand of years have identified angels in slightly different ways. Confusion has run rampant over the centuries, mostly because of the various authoritative sources which conflicted in their opinions and beliefs.

Even in the most ancient societies, there was a wealth of knowledge about the divine beings. Angels were recognized to be as much a part of their lives as humans were.

Then, as now, the spirit beings in the angelic realm were recognized to have personalities with different and various characteristics and responsibilities, thus giving them specific areas in which they live and function.

Each angel was identified according to the responsibility or energy believed to radiate from it; such as the angel of pride, the angel of death, angel of soft winds, angel of the morning star, angel of flowers, etc. Almost everything had an angel associated with it.

Most names of angels were derived from the word in the language of the race or culture where the belief originated. The name meant whatever it was the angel was associated with. In other words, the name of the angel meant what that angel did or represented, such as pride, hope, protector, etc.

Ancient cultures began to give definition to the angels by segregating them into different orders or tribes. Some believed in various choirs, some separated them by a designation of either belonging to earth or to heaven. Some stories talk about the angels' similarities to humans, and some records mention cross breeding among angels and humans. (There are stories of Lucifer or Satan mating with Lilith, the first wife of Adam.) Many people believed that the gods and goddesses in our mythology were angels given human forms. Angels have even been described as beings from other stars or planets.

The names and position of many angels are listed in all scriptures, regardless of which major faith's angelology[2] is studied.

Within the angel realm, angels belong to specific groups. These angelic groups have levels or hierarchies. Historical records show that there were various yet similar hierarchies among

2   In Theology, the study and doctrine of angels.

societies but different designations. Their proximity to God, the Supreme Being, serves as the basis of this division.

The order of ranking of angels is based on the amount of time the angels within that group have been around, and how long they've had to evolve and gain experiences. Additionally, they are classified according to their responsibilities.

None of the levels are better than any of the others. (Angels and mankind are the same in this respect.) God created all things equal and we are all judged on an equal basis. It is mankind who has designated higher and lower ranks to these groups, giving these divine beings designation according to what is perceived to be their direct relationship to God, the Supreme Being.

Theologians have given relevance to the angel hierarchy ranking by their interpretation of the Apocryphal books and ancient scriptures.

In the New Testament, St. Paul writes to the Colossians, in Colossians 1:16: "For by him were all things created, that are in heaven, and that are in earth, visible and invisible, whether they be thrones, or dominions, or principalities, or powers: all things were created by him, and for him."

There are certain variations in names among different religions and theologians. Centuries ago theologians interpreted the angelic hierarchy, giving names and characteristics to the angels in each level, according to their own belief systems and their authoritative source. Most modern day theologians list the different spheres or levels of the angel hierarchy as:

Seraphim

Cherubim

Throne (Ophannin)

Dominions (Dominations)

Virtues

Power

Principalities

Archangels

Angels

All seem to agree that God, the Creator and Universal Force, is above and in charge of all creation, including the angelic realm. Humans and other lower life forms come under the angels.

Under each of these listed angelic designations are separate categories of angels in which angels with lesser power and lesser authority fall within their separate realm. Actual identification of just how many angels are in these separate realms remains still a mystery.

Since modern time and the separation of the dark or fallen angels, there has been an opposite designation and category, with angels of the opposing side within that realm. Remember, though, that God created all things equal and there is nothing lesser in worthiness, just different according to the experiences a being has had.

Most angelologists list the Seraphim and Cherubim as being on the highest level because they have been around the longest. The Cherubim, or Cherubs, are most often portrayed in artwork as childlike in form, although there is nothing in scriptures that indicates angels as being childlike.

The Seraphim appear only once in the Old Testament, in the vision of Isaiah. Isaiah 6:2 states: "Above it stood the seraphim: each one had six wings; with twain he covered his face, and with twain he covered his feet, and with twain he did fly."

Josephus mentioned them in the Book of Enoch (lxxi, 7), "And round about were Seraphim, Cherubic, and Ophannin: And these are they who sleep not, and guard the throne of His glory. (8) And I saw angels who could not be counted, A thousand thousands, and ten thousand times ten thousand, encircling that house."

Angels and archangels are mentioned throughout the scriptures, as are cherub and cherubim. There are only a few references to Seraphim. Other designations are given by St. Paul in his letters to the Ephesians and Colossians in Ephesians 1:2: "...that Christ is raised up ...above all principality, and power, and virtue, and dominion..." and, writing to the Colossians in Colossians 1:16 he says: "In Him were all things created in heaven and on earth, visible and invisible, whether thrones or dominations, or principalities or powers."

The most commonly known Archangels are Gabriel, Raphael, Uriel, and Michael. These archangels have been widely written about over the last several thousand years. Individual angelic names listed in ancient scriptures usually signified their respective attributes.

According to the Old Testament Michael is ranked the highest in the archangel realm. He is considered a leader and warrior in the heavenly ranks.

Jude 1:9: "But even the archangel Michael, when he was disputing with the devil about the body of Moses, did not dare to bring a slanderous accusation against him, but said, 'The Lord rebuke you!'"

Revelation 12:7: "And there was war in heaven. Michael and his angels fought against the dragon, and the dragon and his angels fought back."

In The Doctrine and Covenants of the Church of Jesus Christ of Latter-Day Saints, Michael is spoken of as Adam and the father of all: "And also with Michael, or Adam, the father of all, the prince of all, the ancient of days."

Gabriel is most widely known for being a heavenly messenger. He is the angel credited for bringing the news to the Virgin Mary of the birth of Jesus Christ, and he is also known as the angel that brought the message that subsequently established the Muslim religion. It was the Archangel Gabriel who inspired Joan of Arc to go to the aid of the King of France.

The Archangel Raphael is not mentioned in the Protestant scriptures, but is a healer and helper in the Book of Tobit, within the Catholic Apocrypha. Uriel is mentioned in The Book of Esdras as an overseer of this world and the lowest part of hell.

The Jewish Bible, The Torah, lists 4 archangels: Raphael, Michael, Uriel and Gabriel. The Book of Enoch includes Uriel and Jeremiel. The Muslim Bible, The Qur'an (Koran), names seven, but refers to many. Four archangels are named in the Christian scriptures, most likely handed down through the Torah. Other Apocryphal scriptures mention seven, some twelve, and some many more.

In the Book of Enoch (lxxi 8, 9): "And Michael, and Raphael, and Gabriel, and Phanuel, and the holy angels who are above the heavens, go in and out of that house. And they came forth from that house, and Michael and Gabriel, Raphael and Phanuel, and many holy angels without number."

The most common and popular source of information about angels comes from the Biblical Scriptures.

The word "angel" (singular) appears in the King James Version of the Holy Bible over 200 times in at least 191 verses. The word "angels" (plural) appears approximately 90 times in 92 verses, and the word "angel's" (possessive) appears 2 times in the Bible. The Old and New Testament with the Apocrypha has the word "angel" mentioned at least 240 times and the plural "angels" mentioned over 100 times. The New International Version of the Bible lists the word "angel" a little less than 300 times, "angels" (plural) about 99 times, "angel's" 2 times, and "the angel of the Lord" 91 times. In the references where it refers to "angel," most of the time it refers to the "angel of the Lord." There are other times it appears as "the angel of God" and a few times as "an angel" or "the angel," but most of the time it is "the angel of the Lord." There are slight differences among the various translations of the Bible, but most theologians agree that angels are referenced many times in all scriptures.

Note the following passages:

Psalm 91:11 "For He will give His angels charge concerning you, to guard you in all your ways."

Genesis 16: 7 "Now the angel of the Lord found her by a spring of water in the wilderness, by the spring on the way to Shur."

Mark 1:13 "And He was in the wilderness forty days being tempted by Satan; and He was with the wild beasts, and the angels were ministering to Him."

There are many and varied references to angels in every scripture, however the Bible and other works of literature do not describe or explain in detail what angels are. Therefore, we are left to draw our own conclusions, to form our own beliefs and theories and images.

Some people think that angels are extraterrestrial; that they are here from other planets. I have been assured by messages from angels that they are not life forms from other planets. Extraterrestrials are extraterrestrials, and angels are angels. They are similar only because they both exist in different dimensions and they are difficult for people to identify clearly, and some extraterrestrials come to our aid when we need help, thus simulating the role of angels. Therefore, it is logical that they are sometimes thought to be the same.

As civilizations evolved these ideas and beliefs changed, bringing us down to the Jewish and Christian Scriptures that are more familiar. By that time the versions depicted angels as being on opposite sides instead of being neutral or going back and forth.

CHAPTER 4 -

FALLEN ANGELS

There has been confusion about good and evil angels for as long as there have been studies of angels. Over the years this has raised questions by scholars and laymen alike.

The oldest societies thought of angels as a part of everything and did not separate them into good or bad categories. They were considered similar to humans, trying to please God but faltering at times. Eventually these conceptions evolved into distinct separations of good or evil.

Those angels who are considered evil are commonly known as "fallen angels." One usually assumes them to be demonic in nature. They would be interpreted to be evil, existing in darkness, or even monstrous in nature.

Some of our world religions identify the demons and the angels as being different entities, the demons being a separate type of spirit, an evil spirit, and angels being good spirits not related to demons. Other theologians consider them all the same type of spirits or angels, with some on the dark side. Some relate the two. Some do not; they keep them separate.

After centuries of beliefs that all angels were benevolent workers and messengers of God, literature, philosophers, and theologians began to identify the angel ranked highest next to

God as a fallen angel. There has been much discussion among theologians on where that angel was in the angel hierarchy. Some say he was a Seraphim, some say he was a Cherubim, some say he was an Archangel. But almost all agree that the one considered the most important angel in ancient times fell from grace somewhere along the evolution of angel classification.

The ancient cultures believed that some angels got diverted while performing their duties and did things that were considered evil or went against God's wishes. Some were influenced by other angels to go against God's plan for them. Some angels went back and forth, working both for and against God's wishes. In my research of old records I found it hard to identify which were good angels and which were considered bad, they were so intermingled. The Old Testament does not refer to the fallen angels at all, nor does it indicate or suggest that any angel was evil or wicked.

There are different versions of the "Creation and the Garden of Eden" and the "fall of angels." Many centuries before Christ various stories were told about Lucifer or Shaher (or whoever the mightiest angel was for the particular society telling the story. Some of the names he had during those ancient times were: "Bringer of Light, "Bearer of Light," "Son of the Morning," "Dragon of Dawn," "The Morning Star," "Prince of the Power of Air," and "Satan.") Lucifer challenged the rising sun and lost and was cast down from heaven. Other versions told of Satan becoming angry with God for creating Adam, and leaving heaven, taking many of the other angels with him.

Another version is that Lucifer was the favorite of God. He became jealous when God appointed Lucifer's brother, Jesual, the Son. From his head (thoughts), he gives birth to Sin and, copulating with her, becomes the Father of Death. He is cast out of heaven and renamed Satan-el – meaning "The Adversary." [3]

Several years ago I had encounters with "demonic forces." Through these experiences with the dark side or the negative forces, I learned even more about the supernatural world. Many of my teachers said, "There is no such thing as demons or Satan. They do not exist." They said it was just my imagination, my mind was playing tricks on me, or I must have been going through a stressful time, which brought out negative dreams.

Their teachings reflected the popular theory that demons are created or brought about by the thinking process: When we think negative thoughts, negative things happen. If one chooses, either consciously or unconsciously, to see angels in a negative way, then they could very well appear to be of a demonic nature. In other words, an angel can be monstrous or it can be beautiful, depending on what your thoughts are. Since you create it with your own thoughts, if you sense or see something evil or demonic in nature, change your thoughts to love and beauty and see it change or disappear.

I found that hard to understand. My experience proved to me that they do exist because I saw them with my own eyes, I felt them with my inner senses, and I felt the emotions they brought forth. I decided to make every effort to study these creatures and find out the truth about them.

In my search for the truth I decided to try this method and put all thoughts of evil or fear out of my mind. This concept was hard for me to comprehend and put into practice. I sometimes understood it from an intellectual and conscious level, but when I was faced with fear or uncertainty, it was very difficult for me to

---

3   From "Angels. An Endangered Species" by Malcolm Godwin. Simon & Schuster; ISBN 0-671-70650-0, Copyright 1990

"just believe" and put it into practice. It became easier for me to understand when I viewed it from a scientific viewpoint.

Scientists have come to the point where they can explain this phenomenon – they have proven the connection between mind, body and spirit. Understanding this, we can connect this understanding by remembering that angels are intellectual energy – energy with intellect.

The energy realm of angels does have a positive and negative, because the angels are here on this earth, and the earth is of a negative and a positive nature. There is a duality in this world. There is negative and positive in everything: male and female, AC and DC currents, white and black, dark and light. And there is the negative and positive in the angel world, too. Bear in mind, if there is darkness, there is no light, because if you bring in even the least little bit of light, the darkness is gone. When something is said to be of a negative nature or someone talks about demons or Satan, make the choice to bring in light.

Fear is a strong negative emotion and the opposite of love, which is the strongest positive emotion. If you have fear, that is a type of darkness, a dark energy, and that fear will attract more negative energy. If you think thoughts of love, it will bring in positive energy, and that positive energy eliminates the negative energy of fear.

So, don't be afraid of darkness or angels of darkness, because you can bring in love and light and erase the dark. Bring in love and when you bring that in, there can be no darkness. It is as simple as if someone comes to your door and rings your doorbell and says, "Let me in." You have the choice. You can either let them in or you can leave the door locked, closing them out.

We do have to be careful of how we discern what is right and wrong for us as individuals, and constantly ask God for help in identifying those differences. Our discernment of these energies gets keener with practice, so it is vital that we put it into use every day of our lives.

After I overcame my confusion about the demonic side of the spirit world, I then considered the idea that perhaps I could use these experiences with the negative aspects of the spirit, or dark angels, to help me learn and help me overcome my fears. In my life this theory was correct at least part of the time. In looking back over some of the events in my life when I recognized demonic or evil activity around me, I can say that they were learning experiences that led me into a deeper spiritual life. I thought that if I had not felt compelled to turn to a more active (deeper) spiritual life, I would have continued in a rather mundane lifestyle not really knowing the truth and not being able to help others overcome their fears. Nor would I have had the many wonderful and glorious experiences I have had through my spiritual life – things too wonderful to express in words.

I also understand now that if I had not had negative thoughts and fears, but had been filled with love, none of these negative events would have happened as they did because my attitude and reaction to the events would have been much different. My life would have been filled with wonderful and glorious experiences much sooner.

CHAPTER 5 -

WHAT ARE ANGELS?

There are numerous reports throughout history of angels being seen, but there are about as many different descriptions of angels as there are stories. Because of all the discrepancies, it is difficult to know what angels really are.

Over the years I have read many books and done considerable research on angels. My search has always been for the truth, so I decided to go directly to the source. I asked God to help me explain what angels really are. I was given some wonderful descriptions and explanations of the angelic world, starting with why they were created. Then I was told what they are, so that I could understand it even with my very limited knowledge of physics, and then I was led into knowledge of why they are here.

Angels were created by God to form a connection between the planetary and spiritual worlds. They are energy and light forms with intelligence and memory and were established to assist in the evolution of life forms.

The universe is made up of different energies, and these energies are in definite structure and organization. God is the creator and director of everything, and then the universe branches out from there into what might be called a pecking order of energies.

Angels are a specific type of energy – a divine energy – a form or mass of a specific type of energy that has intelligence and intelligent thoughts. This energy is at a higher frequency, or faster vibration, than our conscious mind. It can be thought of as a raised consciousness or spiritual consciousness.

Love, an energy which radiates in the form of light, is the energy that gives the angels life. It is their source of existence. Angels actually are sparkles of light, or balls of light, made up of the love energy. It has substance, but is unseen.

Angels function and evolve in a manner, through that love energy, that benefits all mankind, and in turn benefits all creation.

This energy is attached to earth through a form of magnetism. It was designed and programmed by God to do nothing more than to serve whomever or whatever it is that it connects with.

Both you and your angel are two intelligent beings – intelligent forces and energy forces – and the two energies (you and your angel) act as a magnet to each other. Each magnet is pulling or attracting (positive and negative polarization). Your human form's energy is the stronger of the two on this plane, and it pulls the angel's essence into your aura or energy field, and it connects.

The angels (these intellectual energies) are attached to individuals, and ultimately connected to everything. The angel essence is always there. It never leaves us. It is part of us, part of our energy field, and it connects - weaving in and out, waving in and out, and undulating.

The angel energy hovers and is in constant motion. It swirls; and as it swirls, that energy moves, and gently moves the mass of energy, leaving a trail behind, similar to a very gentle breeze moving a puff of smoke. That is what gives it the appearance of wings. The angels' wings are a trail of light, similar to a jet stream, whirling and revolving.

Our minds and imagination have created angels with wings. Perhaps centuries ago people saw these in visions or dreams, visualizing what looked like a human form with wings, and they tried to record it by drawing or painting a picture of what they saw. These images were handed down through the centuries as what an angel looks like.

Angels come in all shapes and sizes, and they usually appear in forms that the individual will relate to.

Angels are not put into action, however, until there is a thought or emotion that corresponds to their waves and is strong enough to activate them. They will then manifest in a manner that is beneficial to the individual sending out the intent. This may be done consciously or from a higher conscious level.

They have no emotions, but they have the ability to intellectually reflect emotion. They may appear to be emotional if it will benefit in some way. They express this through us, using our emotions and thought waves.

If you and your angel agree strongly enough, either consciously or unconsciously, your angel will appear in a state or form that you recognize and that you can identify in your mind as a reality in this world.

Angels can influence us and other life forms with their magnetism – the magnetic energy of positive and negative polarization. They are designed to influence us to stimulate a course of action, to move us out of danger, to activate healing, to help us cross over after death, or aid us in whatever way deemed necessary.

When assimilating this information, I realized that if this love energy is magnetic and angels can use their energy to influence humans and other life forms, then angels must have influence on the other light and energy forms that are in the same group of angels, and they all must also influence each other. Working in bands or groups, they are extremely powerful and beneficial.

There seems to be a strong connection to the chakras[4] and the angelic activities or energies. When the angels come in contact with the human body and the human energy or auras, this interaction often energizes or opens and activates the chakras. This experience has been called many different things, depending on the background or religion of the person. The terms and expressions used are usually unique to the particular religious background of the person experiencing it. It has been called Being Anointed by God, Infilled with the Holy Spirit, Baptized in the Holy Spirit, Kundalini, Chi, and Opening of the Chakras – and there are other terms to describe the opening of the human Chakras or energy centers in the body. There are as many different descriptions of it as there are religions or spiritual belief systems.

At the beginning of this writing, I told about an experience I had of a personal contact with an angel. The experience I had at that time was different than Kundalini or the opening of the chakras. The common belief is that Kundalini centers around the head and the heart, whereas my first angel experience affected my mind and whole physical body.

Sometimes, but not always, I have experienced a feeling that is just more than our English language can provide the words to explain. There is usually a feeling of ecstasy and peace and joy. The experience is really so different that there are no words to describe the wonder of it.

---

4   Just as the human body has nerve centers, it also has energy centers, which control the energy flow of the body. These are called chakras.

Grace Johnston

Angels truly are beautiful beings.
Their beauty is indescribable – more than the
human language can fully express.

CHAPTER 6 -

BENEFITS OF ANGELS

Angels are very important to me and play an active role in my everyday life. Everyone has angels, and they play an important part in everyone's life. They are wonderful, beautiful, strong, intelligent companions and helpers; and they are always with us, whether we realize it or not.

Even though angels exist in energy or thought form, they are very influential in our lives.

Angels are worthy beings, and without them we could not exist in the manner in which we do. We would be lost forever in a cycle of existence with no end or beginning. Angels assist and prod us on our way through eternity.

They were created by God to help us. God designed them to benefit us in so many ways – ways too numerous to mention. We cannot conceive of all the ways that angels help and benefit us.

They bring us strength, joy, happiness, and every beautiful and wonderful thing. Their sole purpose is to serve humanity and life forces in other planes so that joy and love can be expressed and exemplified.

They so often come as an answer to our prayers. Since angels are messengers and helpers of God, when we pray, God sends

His angels to help answer our prayers if it is in His design for our ultimate benefit.

They bring us love, peace, and comfort; they help us with our problems, our concern, our joys, and with all things. Angels are necessary for our existence, and we are necessary for their existence. We are together, working and striving for the same love, peace, and comfort. They love us, protect and guide us through our path here on earth and into all eternity.

Without angels we would be robots, probably floundering around in a state of constant dismay, and existing in a world without joy or delight.

Angels create joy. They do not express joy themselves but express through us.

Our being-ness, or just the action of life within us, brings them into active participation with us, and it is with our soul's, or spirit's, permission that angels express their mission. Otherwise they are inactive and on hold until they are summoned.

They connect through our thoughts and emotions, even though they do not feel emotions as we do. They can intellectually, through love, understand our needs and assist us. Much in the same way as a mother's love for her child can anticipate the needs of her children, angels comprehend our emotions and needs, but from a much higher level of understanding that is totally perceived through unconditional love.

Each of us has many angels assigned to us; everyone has his or her own set of angels. There are hundreds sometimes, attached to us by means of the spiritual energy or magnetism. Their sole purpose is to assist us in whatever way we need assistance. They live in pure willingness and eagerness to help us. This is reflected in the Christian bible (New International Version) in Hebrews 1:14, "Are not all angels ministering spirits sent to serve those who will inherit salvation?" and in Psalm 103:19-22, "The Lord has established his throne in heaven, and his kingdom rules over all. Praise the Lord, you his angels, you mighty ones who do his bidding, who obey his word."

Each angel has its unique specific function and responsibility, all of which are many and varied. Some angels are much more active at times, and others more active at other times.

Their reason for existence is to express their duty, which is to assist and benefit those with whom they come in contact and to whom they are assigned.

One angel or group of angels may be assigned to watch over and guide an individual person; another perhaps is to assist our political leaders; another one would be asked to watch over the cities; and so on throughout the universe.

Note: Psalm 91:11, "For he will command his angels concerning you to guard you in all your ways;" and Luke 16:22 "The time came when the beggar died and the angels carried him to Abraham's side." (NIV)

The angels that are assigned to us permanently can assist us in our every endeavor.

I am aware of some of my specialty angels; I try to utilize and make friends with my angels. For instance, I have a Parking Angel. I never worry about a parking place, even at Christmas time. For many years I have always found a space to park my car when and where I wanted one. My friends say that they like for me to drive when we go shopping, because they never have to worry about a parking place. Sometimes it takes a couple of trips around the parking lot to find the right place, especially when I forget to ask ahead of time during a busy shopping season. But I can only recall one time that I didn't get a place where I wanted one. That time the only space available was in the back of the parking lot. I was astounded. I just couldn't believe it! I silently asked, "What is going on?" In my head I heard the words, "You need the exercise."

So, I know if I don't get a parking place when and where I want one, there is a good reason for it. My angels are much wiser than I am and always look out for my needs.

Some of my angels have revealed their sense of humor. Because they are intelligence with memory, they can be humorous as well as wise. (There can be no humor without memory.)

Do you remember a time or event in your life when you were excited about a new idea, or joyously excited about a happy event such as a birth, or purchase of a long-awaited item, or a special occasion? Do you remember the feeling of joy and happiness during that event or circumstance?

It was your angels that helped it come about in such a delightful manner. Without your angels it would have been just another event taking place without joy.

Another one of my angels helps me find lost objects. I call it my Angel of Lost Objects. I often get frenzied when I have misplaced something, but if I remember to calm down and ask my angel for help, I will always find what I am looking for. Occasionally it will take a little time to find it, but it will soon show up, or I will at least know where the object is.

Several years ago I accidentally lost a contact lens. The lens just suddenly popped out of my eye while I was driving home. Since I had worn contacts for many years, this was not a new occurrence for me, so I didn't panic and continued to drive, but adjusted my driving style so I was careful not to disturb the lens wherever it fell. I knew when I got home I could search my clothing and the immediate area around me and find the lens.

Although it was late at night, there was plenty of light from the streetlight in front of my apartment and from the car interior light. I searched for the lens before moving or opening the car door, moving inch by inch over every surface of the car's interior and on my body and clothing. I couldn't find it so I eventually gave up the search, thinking the lens must have slipped down inside my clothing. Very carefully I got out of the car and went inside. After meticulously going over every area of my body and clothing again and again, I still did not find the lens.

The next day I looked again throughout the car before I left for work, but again the search was futile. After I got to work, I asked a co-worker to go out to my car and help me look. We searched and even vacuumed every inch of that car. Still no contact lens. I finally gave up and accepted that the lens must have dropped out of the car when I got out and was lost in the drive where I parked my car, obviously crushed by now.

Luckily my eyes were not so bad that I had to have the lens to see. Sometimes I wore an old pair of glasses or the one lens I had left, or sometimes I didn't wear anything to improve my vision. After three or four months of getting by with that arrangement, I decided I would be able to see much better with new contacts or glasses and it was time to dip into my savings account and buy them. It turned out to be quite a process of getting eye exams and being fitted for lenses, because my eyes had changed so much that I needed bifocals. I had to try several types of lenses before getting ones that fit properly.

At that time in my life, I was also busy in my spiritual life. I was going through transitions in my life and had begun to question and study the reality of God's power and the existence of supernatural happenings.

One day I ended my meditation and prayer time by asking God to give me confirmation of his presence in my life. While driving home that evening I was thinking about angels, and when I got home and reached for the car door handle, my finger hit something. I looked down and saw my contact lens. It was lying in the pocket of the car door where the door handle was, out in plain sight. I was astounded, to say the least. As many times as I had climbed in and out of the car, had the car cleaned professionally and cleaned it myself, there was no way the lens could have been there all those months. And because of the position of the lens, I didn't see any way it could have dropped or flipped into that position without being seen before. The most amazing thing was that it did not seem to be dry or distorted. (For those of you who are not familiar with the old types of contact lens, the lens had to be kept wet, usually placed in a special solution, when they were not in the eye. Otherwise they would dry out and become distorted or warped within a short time.)

I very carefully wrapped the lens in a tissue, took it inside and put it away in a drawer. On my next trip to the eye doctor, I took the lens and asked him to check it out (I didn't tell him the complete story, only that I had lost the lens and just found it). The doctor said the lens was fine, not dry or damaged in any way.

To me it was truly a miracle– that the lens had been found, and that it was still wearable after all those months of being out of solution. I felt it was the answer to my prayer and God had sent an angel to return my contact lens to me. What wonderful confirmation of angelic activity in my life.

I also have a protective angel or group of angels, and I have angels that travel with me. When I go on a trip, I ask my angels to be with me. To protect me and my car, I ask for one on each fender of my car, front and back, and one on each side of the car. Even if I forget to ask, I know they are there.

One particularly busy-traffic day I was on my way to the post office when I was stopped by a red light. I waited for the green light, waited for the traffic to clear, then proceeded to turn left. Just as I reached the middle of the intersection, fully turned to the left with the passenger side toward the oncoming traffic, a truck came flying out of the side parking lot, straight toward me. The driver evidently was in a hurry to make it across the intersection and didn't even looking to see if there was traffic coming. I saw the truck out of the corner of my eye and knew it was coming at a high rate of speed and that it would crash into me. Then, instantly, the truck was on the other side of me, I was fully into the road on the left and the truck was down the street behind me. I pulled over to the side of the road to catch my breath and calm down. I realized that it was a supernatural event that just took place. I believe my angels got between my car and the truck, or perhaps moved one or both vehicles out of danger.

Another time I was turning right into a two-lane street, after stopping and looking both ways, twice. Just as I pulled onto the road a truck went flying by on my left, coming so close that it barely scraped the mirror on my side. There was a passenger in the car with me who told me she had looked, too, and there was no oncoming traffic when I pulled out. She, too, thought that the vehicle seemed to appear out of nowhere; apparently driving so fast that it came upon us before we could see it. I believe my angels were working to protect me then, because if the car had come a fraction of an inch closer, it would have scraped the side of my car in such a manner that it would have caused us to careen into each other, doing much damage. My friend and I stopped long enough to assess the damage and exclaim over the scraped paint on the mirror. We also told our angels how much we appreciated their help and protection.

When I fly in an airplane, I also call on my angels. In the past I've had a fear of flying, but now I just ask the angels, or ask God to send his angels for me: "Please place an angel on each wing, one on the front, and one in the back. Place one below and on top of the airplane. Place angels in the cockpit to assist the pilots, and within the airplane to guide and protect this plane and its crew, and to bless every person on this plane."

Angels will never, never ever work against us, but always for us and for our benefit.

CHAPTER 7 -

THE HEALING POWER

OF ANGELS

One of the greatest benefits that angels bring to mankind is their ability to help rid us of disease and disabilities. The Angels have great healing powers if we will just allow them to help us.

One beautiful spring day when the trees were beginning to blossom into brilliant greens and yellows, a friend and I sat overlooking a park, enjoying the view and a good cup of coffee. Our conversation soon turned to the wonders of God's works in nature and I found myself, as I usually do, telling of my appreciation of angels. My friend joined me in praising the angels in our world, and she told me the following story about one of her experiences:

"Phones were always ringing in my office where I worked. Most of the time the calls were for someone else, but today was my turn and I was called to the phone.

'Hello. This is Tonya Smith⁵' I answered.

---

5   All names are fictitious. The event and details in this story are true.

'Mrs. Smith,' said the kind-sounding voice on the other end of the line, 'Your son Danny is not feeling well. We brought him into the office and he's been lying on the couch for awhile, but he isn't getting any better and has started running a fever. We think you need to come pick him up.'

I quickly talked to my supervisor, called my husband at his workplace and told him I would be picking up Danny. He probably had a cold or some sort of virus that was going around and I would take him home and stay with him.

When I arrived at the daycare center, the minute I spotted Danny I could tell he wasn't just sick. Something was seriously wrong. He was pale and lethargic, not even responding to my appearance in the doorway as I expected him too. Before I left with him, I called our doctor and arranged to bring him directly to the doctor's office before going home.

As soon as we got to the doctor's office, the nurse worked us in right away and got us into a separate room where if Danny had something contagious he wouldn't come in contact with any other patients and affect them.

The doctor interrupted his scheduled rounds and quickly came to check on Danny. He was very friendly and gentle; although Danny was so sick he didn't seem to be aware of much that was going on around him. After a very thorough and complete physical examination, the doctor told me that Danny was a very sick boy, but he did not know what was wrong with him. His advice was to take him home, put him to bed and watch him closely for the next few hours and overnight. If he became worse or wasn't better by morning, we should get him to Children's Hospital in Little Rock, where they might be able to give him additional exams and come up with a diagnosis and solution. Filled with worry and fear, I took Danny home, put him gently in bed and saw that he was warm and as comfortable as possible. He just lay there, lethargic and not caring. It was so emotionally difficult to see him like this. My always-full-of-life, happy-go-lucky baby, now lying there motionless and pale. I could see the sadness in his eyes and it made me sad. I wanted to scream and cry and yell out to God to fix my baby. How could a loving God, if there was such a thing, let a small defenseless child suffer like this? And how could that so-called loving God allow me to suffer because of it?

I gently adjusted the pillows around Danny's head, tucked in the covers so he would be nice and warm, and told him I would be in the living room. If he needed anything, just call me.

When I left the room, I was still having a mental discussion with God. I didn't want Danny to suffer, and he was so sick with some unknown disease or virus or bacteria. Why couldn't the doctors at the clinic here know what was wrong with him? Would his immune system be strong enough to throw it off? - Whatever 'it' was. Would the doctors in Little Rock be able to diagnose his illness and find a cure? I was so scared; scared of losing Danny.

Soon I began to realize just how tired I was. The tension and apprehension was very stressful and I flopped down on the couch, telling myself I needed to get some sleep because it might be a long night. Not being able to get Danny out of my mind, my thoughts went to prayers. I found myself in serious conversation with God, asking God to spare my child, heal him and make him well. I could feel the strong love I had for my son and couldn't help but combine that with the request for God to make Danny well again.

After laying there for a long time, probably dozing for a little while, waking up with the prayers still on my mind, then lightly dozing again, I suddenly heard Danny calling me: 'Mom! Mom! Come here! Mom!' His voice sounded strong and almost desperate. The adrenaline rushed through my body as I imagined him throwing up blood or in severe pain from some unknown source. I rushed into his room, and was very surprised to see him sitting up in bed calling out to me.

'Mom! Mom! I just saw four angels. When I woke up and opened my eyes there were four ladies standing in my room – two at the foot of my bed and two on each side of my bed. I know I was awake because I pinched myself and it hurt. Mom, they talked to me. They said they were angels. They said I will be well and not be sick anymore. And, Mom, you know what? They all looked just like you.'

Danny and I hugged each other and cried some, and he repeated the story over and over. Soon he felt tired again and I left him to sleep. The next morning he felt fine, returned to school while I returned to work.

Danny is now in his 40's. He has never been seriously ill since that fateful day when he was in day care - and in God's care. We never knew what made him so terribly sick, but we still thank his angels and God for sending angels to get him through that difficult time."

What a quick and marvelous answer to prayers!

Whenever we have pain or discomfort, we can automatically release this to God and ultimately to our angels. It is helpful if we realize three things: (1) that we are really spiritual beings. Our spirit and personality is merely being housed in a human form or body. (2) That the human body has been designed to heal itself. If the body gets out of balance, it will not function properly. It needs to be put back into proper balance and it will correct itself, re-establishing perfect health. And (3) since this is just a finely tuned mechanism (housing) that we are using while here on earth, we have control over it; it should not have control over us.

We have the ability to heal ourselves. If we choose to help ourselves, the angels will offer us assistance. They will help and guide us. God's will or desire for us is their desire; therefore, our desire is their desire.

Perhaps our efforts have been weak, but we do not need to cease our efforts to help ourselves, for the angels are with us to help and assist our efforts. They cannot do so without our cooperation.

It is known that not all healing is completed, and some is not done on the conscious level, but since God knows our innermost needs, He often sends his angels to help when we are not aware of it – and always in answer to our prayers. Our prayers are not always answered in a manner that we consciously wish for, but are always answered in a manner that is for our benefit according to God's plan for us.

Please, do not hesitate to pray for help or to request favors from God, so that He can send His angels to help you. Angels are much happier if they can help you or do nice things for you – even to the tiniest thing. You might think, "Oh, I don't want to bother God about this." Please don't think that. The angels' sole function is to help you. If you ask for something, they are delighted. They are working with you and for you all the time, and when you ask for something, it's like saying "Thank you. I appreciate you." When you do verbally or mentally say, "Thank you, I appreciate you." it just makes your life experience so much better. Both you and your angels are happier.

Do not be afraid or ashamed to cry or express your emotions. Sometimes feeling the pain and tears can help heal. Crying helps clear the senses and makes it easier for the angels to work through us.

Sometimes, however, our angels are prevented from helping us. They stay out of our way so we can operate on our own, but it is our ego and our will that influences it to do that. Our conscious mind might rationalize angels into a state of suspension where they are neutral and stagnate. In other words, they can get interference or a block, which would prevent them from acting in our behalf or for our benefit. They will be on hold until the time is such that they can benefit us in some way.

Angels allow us to realize our own power. They were created to assist us, and we merely need to ask for assistance, either consciously or unconsciously. That is why angels assist us even if we do not ask directly – sometimes our subconscious asks for help and that request is projected into our knowing minds.

Angels will never, never ever work against us, but always for us and for our benefit.

CHAPTER 8-

WAYS ANGELS MANIFEST

How do we see angels? Why do some people see angels and others do not? What does an angel look like to another race or culture?

God gave the angels the ability to make themselves known to us if the need to do so is appropriate. It is also a method of giving us a tangible expression of His love for us. We should be very grateful for this marvelous manifestation of one of the mysteries of the universe.

Angels have been portrayed in artwork and scriptures and literary records for as far back as our recorded history shows. Artists throughout the centuries have created angels in a form identifiable through their individual belief system. The identification of angels is as varied as there are different religions or belief systems.

Because each person views things from their own vantage point, governed by their own experiences and education, the perception of angels is also determined by what a person already knows and believes.

Since we live on this planet Earth, we relate to things found on this planet and tend to envision angels as human like in form. Because we know angels to be good and beautiful, we therefore see them as beautiful. On another planet or in some other habitation we might envision them differently, because they are brought into our vision or thoughts through our own points of reference.

Everyone has a variety of angels around them. Each one of you has your own set of angels, and if they appear to you, they will do so in a manner that you as an individual will be able to recognize. Your own creation in your own mind determines how the angels come through to you.

Most of the time angels work around us without us being aware of them, but sometimes angels manifest in different ways. When people report that angels have contacted them, these angels are seen in various forms, and the angels have used many different methods of communication.

Angels might appear in dreams or visions. An angel may appear to you with a message – perhaps a message of assurance and love, or special words of guidance regarding a particular problem in your life, or perhaps a warning to keep you away from danger. It might even be a message about a health problem, one you are not even aware of, or a solution to some health issue you already have. These messages can be very insightful and meaningful in your life.

Sometimes angels communicate through mental telepathy and telepathic insight. In my first mental visualization of an angel, there was a sensing that it was there, accompanied by a mental image. I saw an image in my "mind's eye." It was a large beautiful male form, rather hazy as if consisting of cloudlike material. It was like cotton candy or a heavy fog. It had substance, and yet it didn't have a substance that could be identified. Even though it appeared behind me, I could see it clearly, and I had no doubt that it was an angel. I also knew that it hugged me; I could not feel the physical sensation as one body against another, but I felt the sensation of being hugged and felt a gentle wave of love and peace pass through me. Although it was soft and subtle, it was a tangible experience.

At first I thought it was just my imagination, but then I realized I would not have imagined something like that.

I understand angels from the heart and through my emotions. My angels have appeared to me by manifesting themselves in different ways.

Everyone experiences the presence of angels in different ways. One may even have just a lingering feeling and thought that won't go away that they have sensed an angel or experienced a supernatural event.

Angels have been seen as light, balls or rays of light or light pillars - a huge pillar of light, going up and out into the Universe. They have been seen in human or manlike forms, and some have been described as bigger, more immense than a man, yet in that form or image.

On one occasion a friend called to tell me that there was something or someone in the room with her, but she couldn't see it. She said she knew it was an angel. It was just a feeling and a knowing. She just knew that she knew. As it came closer, it materialized further and she could tell that it had shape and form, but it was like a misty pillar or a mass of light.

Sometimes angels appear as voices. Have you ever heard someone calling you only to realize no one is around?

Sometimes we can just sense someone talking to us, telling us to do or not do something. It usually is heard as an unexpected and unknown voice talking to us. Many people have reported hearing a voice giving them instructions. After following the advice, they later discovered it had saved their life. This was a warning and special guidance from an angel.

When I was a child I would occasionally hear my name being called, and I would run to see what mother wanted. Mother would say she had not called me. Perhaps that voice calling to me kept me from a dangerous situation.

I heard the story of a certain gentleman who was driving a truck through our town. He suddenly heard a voice call out "Stop!" Being puzzled, yet thinking it must have been his imagination, he continued to drive. Again, he heard "Stop!" This time he stopped the truck, wanting to investigate how a very clear voice could come through closed windows above the din of the truck and road noise. He then discovered that something was wrong with his truck and if he had continued, it would have caused a serious accident.

This is just another example of how our angels protect us.

One of the most common sources of recognition of angels is through music. Throughout history authors and artists have depicted angels singing or playing musical instruments. Ancient scriptures declare that the main duty of the angels is to sing praises to God. There are references in Jewish tradition of groups of angels as choirs of angels. The celestial hierarchy for the entire angelic realm probably transpired from this.

John Milton in Paradise Lost wrote, "With bright seraphim and burning row, their loud uplifted angel trumpets blow, and the cherubic host and thousand choirs touched their immortal harps of golden wire with those just spirits that wear victorious palms. Hymn devout and holy songs, singing everlastingly."

Have you heard music but didn't know where it was coming from?

I was told the following story by an Air Force officer: In the final month of World War II an Air Force plane was flying home from maneuvers. The day had started early and had been long and tiring, and everyone on the flight was anxious to get back to base and get some rest. The flight had been a routine flight, but everyone was tired. The sky was clear, with beautiful, fluffy silver clouds scattered below. Suddenly everything was light, a brilliant and silvery light. Then the pilot heard singing. There was beautiful, soft music like a chorus of voices coming from somewhere. But where? They were many thousand feet in the air with no radios that would bring in music. He looked around to see if any of the other crewmembers heard it, and recognized that his co-pilot was reacting in a manner that told him that he had heard the music, too. He instinctively knew that this was the voice of angels.

Angels have been known to have identifiable scents, such as lilac or various other floral scents. Have you ever smelled a sweet fragrance and couldn't find where it was coming from? Many people have reported smelling perfume or flowers when there were no flowers or perfume around. You can walk into a room, especially in your own house, and sometimes sense a floral scent. Maybe it will just be a whiff of it, and then it's gone.

One woman I know says she occasionally smells a particular floral scent upon entering her house, and once she acknowledges and thanks her angel for being there, the scent goes away. Perhaps the angel is just making itself known in order to give assurance and love.

Our own spirit brings about the thoughts of love that angels express. We may not be consciously aware of it, but it's always there on what is commonly referred to as the "subconscious[6]" level. Our energy activates the feeling of love, whether it is a need or request brought through our subconscious or our spirit or from a conscious level.

If the need is felt on a conscious level, that request is sent to our angel through the higher consciousness. Our higher consciousness (subconscious) and our spirit act to attract our angel. This is formed and pictured in our mind, through our brain waves. Pictures of angels are formed in the same way.

Some people recognize the angels' beauty and power through personal experiences.

When an angel makes itself known to us, it will try to contact us in a manner that is comfortable for us.

Sometimes we may have an awareness that the angels are here with us all the time. It is in opening ourselves to that awareness that they become a reality. Once you become aware, or desire to become aware, then the angels can make themselves known to you in a manner you can appreciate and understand.

Each experience I have had with angels has been a little different. And each person experiences angels in his or her own way.

Your interaction with your angels can be as simple or as complicated as you wish it to be.

---

6   The word subconscious is the term with which most people are familiar. The true meaning is higher consciousness because it actually is on a higher spiritual or vibration level.

CHAPTER 9 -

ANGELS IN DISGUISE

Some people say that humans can be angels. How many times have you had someone do something that was really special, and commented that they were "an angel?" Even the biblical scriptures speak of strangers who could be angels.

Divine beings appeared to Abraham in Genesis 18:1-3. "And the Lord appeared to him by the oaks of Mamre, as he sat at the door of his tent in the heat of the day. He lifted up his eyes and looked, and behold, three men stood in front of him. When he saw them, he ran from the tent door to meet them and bowed himself to the earth, and said 'My lord, if I have found favor in your sight, do not pass by your servant.' " (Christian Bible, New International Version.)

In Hebrews 13: 2 we are advised, "Do not neglect to show hospitality to strangers, for thereby some have entertained angels unawares." (New International Version.)

That became very real to me when several years ago (back before the days of cell phones) my young son and I were traveling by ourselves to visit his grandparents. We had gotten a late start that day, but it was still daylight and I thought we had plenty of time to arrive at our destination before nightfall. I didn't want to be on that road at night because it was a dark, lonely road going through the hills in the Ozarks.

Without warning, we had a flat tire. The road was two lanes and narrow, but miraculously we were just approaching one of the few places where the road was wide enough to pull off. Here we were, back in the hills, very little traffic.

I had never changed a tire on a car before and I had real trepidation about this. My son was a young teenager, and he had never changed a tire either. Because the car was a Cadillac, the tires were big and heavy.

We got out of the car and finally managed to get the jack out of the trunk. We struggled with the spare tire, and finally, with both of us working together, we got the tire out of the trunk, too. After figuring out how to use the jack, we eventually jacked up the car. While hoping and praying the car wouldn't fall on either one of us, we got the hubcap off the tire. Then we were stopped. I didn't know what to do after that. Neither of us was strong enough to get the tire off, not even working together.

By then it was dusky dark, approaching nighttime. I was getting scared but I tried to be strong and not upset my son. There was very little traffic on the road, and the cars that passed us refused to stop. Even if they had stopped, could I trust them? I was filled with fear and trepidation because of all the stories I had heard about what might happen to lonely women along the roadside, and about people being attacked by strangers on the road. I was afraid of what might happen if a car did stop. But there were no cars coming by now anyway, so that was another worry. We were miles from civilization. I didn't know what we were going to do.

Suddenly a pickup truck came by. It pulled off the road and wheeled in right beside us. A very nice looking middle-aged man and a young man who looked to be in his teens jumped out of the truck. The man said, "Looks like you need some help." I tried to get some information about him – "Who are you?" "Where did you come from?" The man said he and his son lived in a nearby town and were just passing by. I was too filled with trepidation to communicate well, and without saying much more, the man and teenager started working to change the tire. My son and I just stood there in amazement.

Suddenly I didn't feel afraid any more. We began to talk. The stranger and his son were very polite and kind, but even though we conversed, it never became clear to me who they were or where they came from. When I asked him what his name was, I think he gave me a name, but neither my son nor I could ever remember his name or the town he said they were from. They changed the tire so quickly, yet I cannot remember what tools they used or details of how they did it.

After they fixed the flat, I offered the man money for helping us, but he wouldn't take it. I expressed my deep appreciation. They quickly got back into the truck and drove off. My son and I just stood there looking at each other for a short while, thanking our lucky stars for what had just happened.

We got back in our car and drove on to his grandparent's house and a few days later traveled back to our home. To this day – I don't know who it was that helped us, or where they came from. I just know they were there when we needed them. I have always thought those two strangers were angels.

Many times people have shown up at just the right time to help. Perhaps these helpers are really angels acting through humans. Perhaps our angel asked their angels to influence them to help us at the time we need help, or perhaps angels manifest as humans in order to assist us at a particular time.

A friend called me one night, in the middle of the night, terrified because she thought someone was trying to break into her house. She had awakened and heard someone or something trying to get in her bedroom window. She was very frightened, but had managed to get out of bed, grab the phone and call me. (Why she called me instead of the police, I don't know, nor did she.) I remember praying for her protection and for help. Suddenly, while we were still on the phone, she saw a man's shadow go across a side window moving toward her bedroom. At that moment the burglar or whoever it was suddenly stopped trying to pry the window open and left. We talked for a little while longer until she felt more at peace and then got off the phone. She later told me that she noticed a light on at her neighbor's house and instead of going back to bed, she ran over there. Her neighbors said they had seen someone approach her house on the side of her bedroom, then saw someone else run away. The first man suddenly just vanished from sight. Could that have been an angel that scared the burglar off? She believes that her Guardian Angel had intervened and protected her.

CHAPTER 10 -

MYSTERIOUS STRANGERS

The following story was told to me by a special friend who had a deep spiritual experience:

"We had moved to Ohio shortly after our second child was born. I did not work because the children were still babies, so my husband worked as a bartender on Saturday nights at a local roadhouse to supplement his regular income. Tonight I needed a break just to get out of the house, so I went with him. Unfortunately, in addition to tending bar, John sampled too many of his bar drinks, and by the end of the evening it was obvious that he had had too much to drink. He became melancholy and sentimental, and when the bar closed he wanted to take me to his old home place and show me where his family used to live. He insisted on driving, and I finally gave in because everyone else had left the area and I knew it was the only way I could get home. In spite of everything I could do, John drove about 30 miles away from our home and our children, barreling over the snow covered roads. This was January in Ohio. It was seasonably cold, with a frozen blanket of deep snow covering everything. Nothing was moving as far as my eyes could see. The night was silent.

We finally got to his destination about 1:00 a.m. John pulled into a narrow country lane. I could tell that no cars had been on this road because the snow was still deep and unmarked. Within just a few feet after we left the highway, we slid into a deep ditch and were immediately enveloped in the deep snow.

We were trapped, and no amount of cursing or wishing could take the snow away and place the car and us up on the road again. My husband John and I were alone in the car, stranded on a lonely country road in the Ohio countryside.

My body was seized with pain as fear shot through me and combined with the bitter cold. My thoughts went to our two young children who were at home with the babysitter. Are our children okay? Will we freeze to death and never see them again? We don't even have a blanket. Who will take care of them if we don't survive? We have to get home.

A flicker of light on the sequined snow brought a faint reminder of God's beauty in nature and my belief in God. I immediately started praying.

The door on my side was completely blocked by the snow, but somehow John managed to crawl out on his side and walk back to the highway.

He had only been on the side of the road for a few minutes when a car stopped. It was a brand new Ford and looked like it had just come off the assembly line, perfectly clean, no markings of any kind. There were two men in the car. They asked my husband what was wrong and he told them our situation. They said they could not help get the car out of the ditch but they would take us home.

John quickly accepted their offer. He then rushed to our car and with much effort managed to pull me out through the driver's side.

We went back to the highway and got into the car with the two men. They were dressed very inappropriately, especially for this time of year and in this part of the country. They wore three piece suits and hats. I did not see heavier coats or clothing anywhere in the car. They had fine features. Their skin was so smooth and clear that I thought they had no whiskers at all. If one may call men beautiful, I would say these were beautiful men.

They talked only briefly before we left in their car, just enough to gather information about our dilemma. Finally as a way of being sociable, I asked where they were headed. The man on the passenger side turned to tell me that they were from Cleveland on their way to Columbus. The men seemed very reluctant to talk so that was the extent of the conversation. The rest of the trip was in total silence, but I experienced a feeling of peace and tranquility that stayed with me the rest of the night.

I thought the men were exceptionally nice, but I thought it was unusual for them to be traveling in this weather at two o'clock in the morning on a little-traveled highway. What was even more phenomenal was that their car remained clean, even though the roads were slushy from the ice and snow.

When we got to our house, they waited while John brought the babysitter out so they could take her home. John went with them, and when they returned, we offered to pay them for their help. They refused to take any money. This too, struck me as remarkable. These perfect strangers had appeared out of nowhere, in the middle of the night, had gone out of their way to help us, and would not take anything as reward for their kindness.

I was so thankful to God for his divine intervention in our crisis. We would have frozen to death before morning and our two babies would have been orphans if these two strangers had not come along just at the right time to help us.

Over the years I have thought about this incident and the oddity of the whole sequence of events. Could these men have been angels sent in answer to my fervent prayers for help? Or were they beings of another kind? God sometimes answers prayers in mysterious ways."

CHAPTER 11 -

COMMUNICATION

FROM ANGELS

Since that first "hug" from an angel, I have had many experiences and personal visits from angels. There were times when they gave me specific messages. At other times, they merely made their presence known, either through vision or sensory perception. Sometimes they came to comfort me when I was feeling particularly stressed or lonely, and other times they came in answer to a prayer and request from me. No matter what the reason for them making their presence known, I have always been very grateful and appreciative. Each experience has been wonderful and enlightening.

Over the years I have gone from an academic knowledge of angels to a wonderful awareness filled with personal experiences.

My spiritual, or supernatural, experiences are very similar to what other people have experienced. The awareness of angels has been revealed in stories going from one human being to another; sometimes in whispers and doubt, sometimes in awe, and always in excitement and wonder. People are having personal experiences with angels, and they are recognizing their beauty and power, as evidenced by all the new artwork and literary works expressing the angels' uniqueness.

This awareness of angels has become a normal part of many people's lives. This phenomenon of angelic recognition seems to be considered by modern-day spiritual minds as being part of the process necessary in the evolution of man.

It seems only reasonable to question just what will be next. What could move us to a higher level of thinking? What could be greater than angels?

The answer came to me directly through God's messenger, an angel. The answer was, of course: <u>communication</u> from the angels. Now that people have been made aware of the existence of angels, these angels will now communicate with us.

Communication with an angel came as quite a surprise to me.

Christmas of 1992 found me in a financial crunch. I wanted to buy gifts for my friends, but I didn't have the money to purchase something special for them all. I knew they would understand if I did not get them anything, but nevertheless I really wanted to give them a special gift to let them know I thought about them often and how much I cared about them.

Since I am creative and artistic, I decided I would make gifts for everyone. I could not think of anything appropriate and my creativity was not working when it came to coming up with ideas.

One late afternoon I was meditating and praying about this. I asked God to give me an idea for an inexpensive, yet meaningful gift that I could make for each of my friends. While I sat there – very relaxed and almost asleep – words started flowing through my mind and then sentences started forming. After a minute or two, three or four sentences had floated through my head. I suddenly realized what was happening, and in the same moment I realized that these words were coming to me from beyond my conscious mind. I rushed to find a pencil and paper and began writing the message down. When the emanation of words stopped, I had captured about forty verses.

When the angel spoke to me, it was as if a person was speaking to me and I heard the words in my head, as opposed to hearing them from an outside source. I copied them word for word, exactly as I understood my angel speaking to me, as the words came into my mind. At the same time the words came into existence, I was also feeling the meaning of the words. It was easy for me to translate their meaning, because the sense or understanding came through to me at the same time the words were formed.

The sentences were worded in a manner that was not what I would have consciously written. It just simply wasn't my style, and I did not think that I had the ability or talent to create anything of this nature. Without a doubt, the message had come from God. Then later I realized that it must have come through an angel, since angels are God's messengers.

These are just a few of the verses given to me at that time, and as you can see, the style is poetic, and very wise and loving:

Love is more power than anything envisioned. Love – If all is done for love, great things will happen. Unite with love – not self love, but love for all concerned. All is love, joy and peace. For that you love.

Your source of supply comes from God. As your Source of Supply dictates, your needs will be met. Therefore do not spend time worrying or fretting. See happiness in everything you do and it is done for you.

Judge not that you be not judged means to give others freedom of behavior and thought so that you also may have freedom. It is uncomfortable to feel pressured or judged before other men.

The power of prayer is useless unless the thought behind it is sincere. Not every person or living thing is ready for perfection. Correction is available for everyone but not deemed appropriate for all.

The greatest honor is to serve. It is through serving that one is honored.

See the beauty in all the world. The world is in turmoil but there will be peace in your heart and in the heart of any man who chooses to walk with God.

I considered typing these verses and making copies for my friends. But the next morning I had an inspiration to create something with a clock that made a connection between angels and making time in the day for meditation to commune with the angels. While shopping for inexpensive clocks, I happened to see a little hourglass, priced at only a dollar. I purchased hourglasses for each of my friends. At home I created tiny pages containing one verse each. I wrote another page, which expressed the blessings from the angels and their hope that the recipient would find time to spend with the angels' thoughts. I put the pages together, and then tied them to the hourglass.

With angelic help I created a Christmas gift that was truly inexpensive yet very, very meaningful.

Over the years the angels have added to those original forty verses. From that collection I selected 60 verses and created a journalized book called Celestial Inspirations—Thoughts from Beyond the Intellect (ISBN # 0-9741118-0-5). It has been a special gift of inspirational thoughts for new friends I have acquired since then.

After this mystical experience with an angel talking to me, I learned how to initiate communication with them through a type of mental telepathy.

Some of the angels I have communicated with have never identified themselves to me. Most of the time I ask for an angel's name, but sometimes I do not because I am more interested in the information they want to impart rather than learning their identity.

This is a message I received from one of those angels:

Angels are now here to visit us on an intellectual level. Their resources take them into all elements and places in the universe.

(Humans) have been selected to communicate with the angels. Each one (angel and human) is divine. (Because) The energies are compatible; each person is selected or chosen (for this experience). The angels are magnetic and we are energized through this experience.

There is Oneness with all creation. Angels bestow on each person their divine energy, pulling extra (from God, The Universal Force), as it is needed, and extending extra energy through them, into each divine source of redeemable quality[7] energy beings. Their source of energy is from the Universe. They pull, as they need it.

It's really a simple activity, but one that is commonly misunderstood. Angels and people can connect if the intent is sincere and clear enough for the angels to know that you really want to communicate with them. If you are sincere and your intention is to make contact with an angel for a good and beneficial purpose, then you will be successful. Your spirit will bring it to you.

---

7   Some beings are not compatible with specific angelic energies. Although we are all a creation of the universal force (God), there are some entities/energies that have been distorted in nature and cannot be redeemed in the same lineage as originally designed. These distortions come from entering different atmospheres at times of evolution. Thus the sequence of events has caused the distortions.

They will be able to make their presence known as long as you and your angels have the same vibrations or thought patterns.

In order to receive messages from angels, our vibration must be on the same wavelength as the angels', much like tuning in to a radio wave or frequency. This vibration is the energy that emanates from everyone and these vibrations can be adjusted by thoughts. Thoughts are waves of energy and the waves create vibrations. If thought waves are changed, the vibrations are changed.

An angel can be thought of as a form of intelligent energy that tunes in to your thoughts, just like you would tune a radio or a TV to a specific frequency in order to produce sound or form a picture. Angels pick up our thoughts, and if they are on the same wave length or frequency, we will be able to communicate with them.

Should you choose to communicate with an angel, the angel will meet you halfway, trying to accommodate you by connecting in a manner that would be recognizable to you. The angel will talk to you, usually through mental telepathy, in a way that you will understand. If you speak in English, the angel will adjust to your English vocabulary. Likewise, if your native language is Spanish, the angel will communicate in Spanish. Whatever your language of communication, the angel will comply. Because the communication is through thought waves, the message or manifestation is understood in your own thoughts – just as a computer picks up information in a particular language according to the program installed in the computer hardware. The angel will relate to you as an individual.

There have been many times that angels have given a message to someone without the person consciously being aware of wanting it to happen. It is at those times that the individual's spirit, through the subconscious mind ("subconscious" being a higher consciousness level), causes the individual to be open to and aware of the angels and/or their message.

Sometimes an angel will put words into your head and you will hear messages, just like someone is talking to you. You will hear the words, not from an outside source but just in your mind. At other times there will be thoughts interjected and you will just know what the angel is trying to convey. It will be an inclination and a feeling of knowingness.

And almost always, the angel will give you a wonderful feeling of being loved and protected –a spiritual hug.

Over the last several years I have visited with many different angels, including Archangels Raphael, Gabriel, Michael, and to an angel who identifies itself as Joycelyn or Jocelyn, a leader of a choir (group or family) of angels. I also talk with my personal angel, Janimaca, the one who acts as intermediary between me and other angels and who helps me communicate with others.

I still remember the first time I contacted my personal angel and became acquainted with her. It was such a delightful experience, filled with joy and love. There was also a feeling of amazement that I could actually do such a thing.

CHAPTER 12 -

PURPOSE OF ANGELS

Since the angel realm is a hierarchy, it is only logical that we have an angel who is in charge of and directs our other angels.

Angels have different responsibilities, and each of us has a particular one with the responsibility of acting as the mediator among all of our angels. If you, in the conscious level or third dimension level, need help or contact with an angel, your own directive angel, the one connected to you individually, will get in contact with the angel or angels that can help you with your specific need.

You may or may not be aware of that process.

Sometimes I ask to talk to a specific angel, usually one that I consider the dominant angel in a group, such as one of the archangels. At other times I ask to talk to my personal angel, or perhaps one who can help me with a particular problem. I have always had this request granted and have gained access to the specific angel that I ask for.

At times when I communicate with an angel that can help me with a particular concern, the angel usually does not identify itself by name. I just feel its presence – a warm, gentle spiritual hug – a wonderful feeling of love, security, and peace of mind.

Although in the higher realms earthly names are not important, in this earthly realm names are important to us. Therefore, an angel can have a name if you want it to have a name. The angels understand our need for clarification and will give us a name that we can identify them by. It also helps us identify with them more closely.

When I asked my personal angel for her name, she told me her name is Janimaca. Her name is female because I sense that she is female and view her in my mind's eye as a beautiful female essence.

Because angels are spirit and intellectual energy, they actually are neither male nor female. I simply decided that I wanted a female angel, so that's what I have. If tomorrow I change my mind and want a male angel, I can do that and it will be manifested. But the essence or information received would not change.

During one of my conversations with Janimaca, I asked her to tell me about herself. This is part of her message, exactly as she told it to me:

Angels are beings, light creations, thoughts. They are life form; sources of strength, power sources; thought that can be changed; resources drawing or pulling from each other if needed; unit, and unity; bands of light and energy; sources of power; thoughts of beauty, strength, peace, joy, light, happiness, humor, laughter; evolving in divine energy that heals the Universe and strengthens the creation of light energy sources. They appear in the form in which you can assimilate it, or them.

All (angels) have intellect. All are love. They are made up of love, joy, peace, and divine energy. They direct and lead similarly to the nerve cells in the body that direct other parts of the body for a specific function.

The angels have come to serve you. There is always one more adept, more stable, more experienced, higher spiritually, who can act to protect and guide. This is done with love.

Our mission in life is to be of service to mankind and help him evolve into the greatest creation he can be. When he has evolved through eternities, then he will become a powerful creative power itself, creating other universes and becoming greater and greater throughout eternities. The power is fulfilled as all become one in the universe with the creator.

CHAPTER 13 -

A MESSAGE FROM ANGELS

If you do not by now believe in angels, then perhaps you can accept the words in this chapter, and all previous words written by the angels, as beautiful prose written in an altered state of mind allowing literary freedom.

This message is for everyone, whether one considers the source believable or not.

"Love is the most important thing in this universe. It is the key to all success. All endeavors should be glorified and honored with love.

(Have) Dedication to each other. Be devoted to learning how to love and how to express love - Raising your vibration rate to the point that you can go beyond (what you know). Raise yourself above and beyond this third dimensional state or this worldly state. Raise yourself above all the violence and the cruelty, and the confusion and the chaos, the tension, the anger, the hatred. These things have their place, but they have served their purpose, and now it is time to move beyond that. Learn each lesson as you go and realize that these former things must be laid aside for newer things, evolving into a world that is nothing but love and understanding and wisdom.

Your (Our) definition of wisdom is love combined with the understanding that comes through total acceptance of everyone being as one in God and in a relationship with the universe. Each thing was created for its own purpose and has evolved and developed to this point and is where it is supposed to be in its creation. It will move from this point to another point, as all things are evolving.

With love you can create, and can change things. You can be whatever you want to be as long as love is the intent and the key factor and the motivation - true love, unconditional love, a love that is totally accepting, totally without fear, having total devotion to the heavenly Spirits, the higher energy forces, and the higher energies.

Love yourself, love all of your brothers and sisters, love everyone. Love all of life, all of creation, love every animal, every insect, love everything that exists, knowing that everything has its place.

God created it all. All (was and is) created by and through love. All things were created for good and for the existence of all. Each one should be respected and identified and recognized as having their place in your society and in your universe and know that each one has their own purpose and has the right to be here just as you do, no matter what color or design, no matter what their purpose. They each have their own individual needs and their own individual purposes. And love is respecting that and identifying that, as individual selves, and yet as all in one.

Identify yourself with all of the universe. See yourself in the universe, see your place in this society, and know that you are just a drop in the ocean that works and moves and makes up the whole.

Your part is very important and could not be done without you, and each one of us is equally important. Each individual spirit is like a drop of water in the ocean. There are some that make big splashes, and at times others make big splashes, but we all move and work as one and each of us has our own place and our own identity.

Love must be recognized as the identifying factor that activates all things. Without love there could be no existence in this universe, but with love anything is possible, and it will eventually evolve into the higher dimensional level of a higher vibration and raise each and every one of you to a much higher level, which is one that exists without chaos or greed or anger or hurt or frustration or any of the things that you tend to identify with now. There will be nothing but love and peace and harmony and beauty, and grace, and an angelic existence, in the place which you call Heaven. It will be for all. All will exist in that plane, in that level, and in that level of vibration and energy, and all will be at peace. It will come about in its own time because in the higher realms there is no time (as we know time).

Lay aside your worldly cares, your worldly desires. Concentrate on love, learning how to love and express love, not of the world, but of the Spirit and through the Spirit. And you can be a part of this wonderful creation that will be (to) your advantage and in your space and time. This time that you have created is very illusive, as it is supposed to be, and when it is filled with love, it will be no more. There will be no time.

Love is the most powerful thing in this universe. It is what Jesus came in to teach, to tell you about. All the other entities that came into this hemisphere to teach have all been directed by love. Love is the greatest power in this universe. It will be known throughout the history of all universes as one of the greatest things that takes place.

There are other emotions and other thoughts that direct and motivate and create in other universes, but in this universe and this galaxy, love is the ingredient and the energy that has the most power. It is the key to everything.

Your needs are our needs, your wishes and desires are our wishes and desires. We are all as one. All needs are the same; all desires are the same. They are just viewed from different levels, different angles.

There are different interferences, different influences, but all needs and desires and wants are the same. Your existence is our existence.

Bless you one and all. Bless you creatures of this universe, living beings, light beings. You are so beautiful in our eyes, our vision. We love you dearly.

Thank you, and bless you all."

CHAPTER 14 -

WHAT'S NEXT?

We are experiencing more angelic activity at this time because of the changes that are taking place in the Universe. These transformations are happening around the Earth and within the Earth.

Our universe was designed to evolve. Our Earth is evolving within our universe. We are evolving into a higher dimension. We (humans) are ourselves rising to a higher level, into the fourth plane (dimension) and a higher spiritual level. In that process many of us are becoming more open and thus are more aware of the angels.

Instead of evolving in a peaceful and harmonious manner, our cultures have continued to abuse and misuse our environment and each other, even though throughout history mankind has been given warnings from many different sources. Much of this information can be substantiated by discoveries in ancient documents, hieroglyphics, and scriptures. Because mankind has not heeded these warnings and corrected itself in order to rise to a higher spiritual level, we are at this time in history going through a transition stage, which will be uncomfortable and sometimes violent.

The earth is going through difficult times right now and events are happening at a faster and more dramatic rate than ever before in recorded history. These changes can be considered through religion and science.

Various religions consider the changes that are taking place as "Armageddon," the "end times," or the "Time of Great Change," which is mentioned in all scriptures. Every religion known to man has mentioned a time when everything will change, resulting in either being destroyed or being changed to a different structure.

From a scientific viewpoint, there are changes and shifts taking place in the universe that astronomers and scientists are now discovering, and they are scientifically recognizing how one thing affects another.

The magnetic grid of the earth is shifting, causing varied phenomena. Because the ozone layer is changing, the earth's atmosphere is changing, thus causing weather variances, earthquakes, warming trends, and other environmental changes. The magnetic changes also misalign the intuition of some of the animals causing migration patterns to become confused or animal instincts to deviate from their normal patterns.

Even if we are not consciously aware of it, mankind, animals, and all living things are feeling the effects of the earth's changes in some way or another.

It is important at this time in our earth's existence that mankind work together to save our species and the universe we live in. We cannot do this alone (as history has shown) and we need all the help we can get. That's why angels and other spiritual and metaphysical intellectual energies have come into the earth's atmosphere in a more identifiable manner. They are all here to help us through this transition.

Will you cooperate with them?

###

"The angels are here to serve you."

OTHER BOOKS BY

GRACE JOHNSTON

CELESTIAL INSPIRATIONS – THOUGHTS BEYOND THE INTELLECT

Inspirational poetry and prose dictated by personal angels and a unique angel from Pleiades.

ANGELS – THOSE WONDROUS BEINGS

A beautiful, entertaining and educational book of inspiration and hope. Whether you believe in angels or not, you will enjoy reading about angels, what they have to say to us, and stories of visits by angels.

OUR CREATION AND DESTINY
BOOK ONE – CHARTING THE HEAVENS

Reveals the mysteries of our creation and the secret of survival in these difficult times. Explains the creation and makeup of our universe and life forces, parallel universes, and alternate selves. Learn about yourself, your purpose and destiny.

Forthcoming Books by Grace Johnston

MY SOUL'S JOURNEY HOME

The spiritual memoirs of Grace's personal growth leading her to higher knowledge and to the discovery of life on the many planes of existence. She shares her knowledge and personal experiences of spiritual, metaphysical and paranormal activity.

THE WORLDS WITHIN

A documentary on the universes within our universe. Personal experiences with vivid descriptions of the many planes of existence.

OUR CREATION AND DESTINY
BOOK TWO – OUR SPIRITUAL FAMILY

Discover how you can access the higher reaches of the mind and gain higher knowledge. Become acquainted with your higher selves to fulfill your purpose and destiny. Learn how to resolve difficult issues, bring more happiness into your life, and learn restorative healing techniques.